IT'S NOW OR NEVER

Free Thoughts of a Psychotherapist

www.dorakiki.com

London.uk

Publisher ©2021 Dora & Kiki Ltd

Author ©2021 Oscar Travino

Illustrations ©2021 Various Authors

DORA & KIKI
Publishing Company

It's Now or Never

Table of Contents

It's Now or Never

Preface

It took almost three years to collect thoughts, to understand where to start, and, above all, to figure out if I actually had something to say.

To give.

I have the priceless luck of doing a job that I love, and that leads me to look out on the intimate and wonderful windowsill of many people.

Lots of souls.

There are fantastic worlds within each of us.

There are truths to be discovered and horizons to be overcome.

And a million thoughts that every day appeared on my mind, asking to be fixed in black and white.

I did it.

For myself.

Because it's like keeping a logbook.

A black box of existence.

For those who want to read them.

Because sometimes, a thought can touch hidden chords of the soul, making them vibrate and awakening that part of us that we no longer knew we had.

Let's go.

Leave the dead weight of your ideas and fasten the seat belts of your soul. Listening.

Because with her, you will always be safe.

Have a safe trip.

Because to go fast, you can be alone.

But to go far, you have to be together.

I wrote this book because I trust people.

Yes, trust.

My work inevitably leads me to encounter the emotional and intimate world of many lifetimes.

Magnificent worlds, made of light, ideas, passions, fears. Incredible shades of enchanting beauty.

I believe that so much of our suffering is the product of our Ego. A self-referential structure that leads us to perceive the world with unique and unrepeatable lenses, ours.

And then it is *I* who suffer, it is *I* who feel, it is *I* who think, it is *I* who say, it is *I* who remain silent, it is *I* who believe.

I, I, I.

Closed universes.

And we feel alone, different, and misunderstood. Inner worlds and shades of enchanting beauty that we do not show.

It is as if we lived a total disconnection between the private of our minds and the social. The dialog (from *dia*—through, and *logos*—speech) becomes —ego-log—.

Speeches made within one's own mind without confronting them with the objectivity of reality. With the other.

But without openness, there is no growth or union. We are together, but without feeling each other. Each closed in own self-representation that makes us feel so unique, distant, and misunderstood. And no. I don't know about you, but I'm not doing this.

The era of maximum speed and many opportunities, on the internet, Facebook, chats, social networks, smartphones, is paradoxically the era in which we feel most alone.

Isolated.

And we desperately need to go back to the essence of things, to our nature.

I trust people.

Sometimes, while listening and experiencing the emotions and words of those in front of me, I unintentionally relate them to those heard by someone else, maybe a few hours before.

So I think, "but why don't they meet? If only they saw each other, really."

If only we let ourselves be seen. If only we broke the closed ego loops for a moment and really met the other. A moment's meeting would sweep away the veil of all deadly loneliness and misunderstanding.

I trust people.

Because I know that revolutions start with minor changes that spread relentlessly and slow. The butterfly effect, they call it. The flapping of a butterfly's wings causes a hurricane on the other side of the world.

I trust people.

And in those shades of enchanting beauty that we treasure so intimately.

I know that part exists, and I know that's where we can plant the seeds of change.

Because I know it's not true that we're happy with it.
I know it's not true that everything is off. I know it is not true that we have stopped believing, feeling, dreaming, wishing.
I know we have fears and dreams that are too similar not to meet.

Me, you.

We are human beings.

Flesh, blood, soul, emotions, fears, desires, and sighs.

—We are such stuff as dreams are made of—, wrote Shakespeare.

Too similar to be so distant.

It's Now or Never

Chapter I

I

Your life does not change

without transforming oneself.

[Simone de Beauvoir]

I lived in the same house for 36 years, on the sixth floor of a building with a lift. That elevator, a gateway to the outside world, or a return to the warmth of my home. Twenty-seven seconds of descent.

There, dominates the embarrassment of the ascents shared with the residents (it seems that everyone is looking for or rattling the keys in those interminable seconds) and a large mirror.

A mirror that saw me tanned, tired, energetic, impatient, euphoric, scared, cold, sleepy, in love, desperate, joyful, with bags under the eyes, elegant, wrinkled.

About a month ago, someone decided (I don't know who) to apply large leaf-shaped green stickers on that mirror.

There.

The first time, I had a start in the unexpected surprise of perceiving, at the opening of the doors, a structure of colors and shapes different from the one so imprinted in my consciousness. The image seen thousands and thousands of times.

Four weeks have passed, and even today, when those doors open, I have that little gasp of surprise.

An image so deeply fixed struggles to adapt to a new shape.

And then I thought about what happens in relationships.

How extraordinarily intense can the (in) voluntary force that pushes us to see things, and people, always the same, can be. A reassuring repetition, an immutable basis that reassures a lot. The unexpected destabilizes, frightens. But the risk is to become blind to a world that, in reality, is constantly changing.

My partner is not always tedious, heavy, resourceful, selfish, generous. My friends, my parents, my co-workers are not.

It is not the same the light that every morning caresses my window, the pillow, the sheets.

My cat is not the same, the car I use to go to work, the front door, my shoes aren't.

My clothes, my expression, my mood, my desires are not the same.

—But I've been to the hairdresser, and you don't tell me anything?—

—Didn't you notice I lost weight?—

—I bought that new outfit for you—.

How many things do we not see for that stubborn and unconscious desire to perceive everything always equal to itself?

Let's look.

Beyond preconceived ideas.

Beyond self-assurance, that becomes stagnation.

Let's really look.

There is part of me that wants to perceive that mirror the same as itself, like a kind of perceptual habituation that makes me have a little jolt whenever the doors are opened. I am faced with something unexpected. And all this because someone (I don't know who) arbitrarily decided to apply those stickers.

Thank you, unknown benefactor.

Now I open my eyes, I really look.

And I am amazed, every time.

There is no way to happiness,

happiness is the way.

[Thich Nhat Hanh]

A strange thing happened yesterday.

I was on my bike, under a sky full of clouds.

The strong wind, the sea foamed strong waves on the rocks. I was headed to Gallipoli.

And that's how, pedaling, I got a feeling.

Clear, sudden, immediate like an idea.

I felt slow.

Now, a mountain bike on a flat road, in seventh gear, travels at a speed of around 40 km/h.

And I felt *slow*.

So, I asked myself, "slow compared to what?" Maybe a car, a motorcycle. But what is the parameter that measures being slow or fast? 40 km/h is a faster speed when the vast majority of living beings move.

I was fast, yet I felt slow.

So, I thought about how addicted we are to a time-no time that pushes us, now in a completely automatic way, to want to run.

Get there right away.

The goal, more than the journey itself.

And yes, I fear that the same thing happens about human relationships as well. Work, loved ones, relationships, goals.

Wanting everything at once means losing everything.

And then I swerved towards the cliff.

I abandoned the bike on the rock.

The sky full of clouds, the strong wind, the waves decided on the rocks.

And I stopped to look at the sea.

The sea has a lot to say, to teach us.

It never feels slow. It doesn't care if its waves are fast, high, foamy, or dark.

It is like that.

It is himself. Only that matters.

It loves itself as it is.

Sometimes fiery and dark,

at times flat and shiny.

It is there, lying on the back of the world with the only infinite joy of looking at the sky and falling in love with it.

Everyday.

You cannot be unhappy when you have this:

the smell of the sea,

the sand under your fingers,

the air, the wind.

[I. Némirovsky]

I walked towards the sea, slowly, absently, now aimlessly.

The silence around me. It was morning, and there was no one in the streets of the city.

I was about to turn back when I stared ahead rather than at the ground.

I wondered why all that beauty.

She was there, practically forever. And it persisted.

Beyond my looks, my winters, moods, or races through the folds of my commitments.

She was there. Immovable beauty.

—There is a sunset a day—, I told myself, and then I wondered how many I had really seen.

Maybe 100, maybe 300, maybe more, maybe less.

I wondered why all that beauty.

And then I realized that the answer was me.

It was there for me.

To remind me that no matter how desperate, tired, busy, inattentive, dissatisfied, or sad, I am.

There is always an elsewhere, of light and beauty, there waiting for me.

It is there for you.

You have your legs to move,

and your eyes to marvel again.

If you don't know,

that's what life is made of,

don't lose the now.

I was one of those who never go anywhere

without a thermometer,

without a hot-water bottle,

and without an umbrella and without a parachute;

If I could live again,

I'll try to walk bare feet

at the beginning of spring

till the end of autumn.

[J.L. Borges, Instants]

Of Instants

Today I parked the car quite far away. I walked the long way to my studio, the air rather cold, a gloomy sky, dark clouds. Omen of rain.

At that moment, I thought of the two umbrellas I had in the car (there for a long time, residues of ancient rains). Now. After a moment's loss, I reflected that it is not just a mere forgetfulness. I knew I had those umbrellas. There. The question is another.

The thing is, I never take an umbrella before it rains. Never.

I believe it is something other than a habit or disorganization. It is a mental attitude.

The fact is that I always start with the idea that it won't rain and that if it does, I could take shelter, wait, run. At most, get a little wet.

But NOW it's not raining, and I don't feel I need to take precautions—just in case—.

I'm here now.

And I've always thought that situations must be addressed when and if they occur. Now I know someone will turn up their noses. It may seem strange, naive, irresponsible, or whatever. But this mindset has always saved me. Yes, saved.

From small and superfluous anticipations, worries, expectations.

Sometimes I waited for stopped raining while drinking a coffee or, if lucky, leafing through pages in a bookstore. Or exchanging a few words with a tourist at the foot of a statue in the center of Rome. A few times, I got wet. And the rare times it has happened, I assure you that I got away unscathed, at most with a few sneezes.

I think it will rain and I take an umbrella. I think my partner can cheat on me, and I start controlling him.

I think I might lose my job and start working with tension and anxiety.

I think I might develop a disease and start living in anguish.

The truth is that no one knows if and when, and there remains a single truth, unsettling in its simplicity; we are alive, here, right now.

And that's enough.

And perhaps we can choose not to allow hypotheses, anticipations, and fears of an unknown tomorrow to steal some of the colors of our today.

And then I continued my way under that dark sky, the cold air on my face, my footsteps, and my breath.

And I smiled at my now.

It's Now or Never

An-al Generation

I belong to an an-al generation.

Sodomized, underestimated, stuck.

An-al.

Between *an*alogic and digit*al*.

The middle ground between two codes.

Analogic derives from the Greek *analogous*— proportionate—, —similar—.

There is a sender, a message, a receiver, and each passage is marked by equivalent measures.

I know *how* much it is because it is as *much* as it is.

A second is the click of a hand on the quadrant. The red 37 on the thermometer is the borderline between the backpack and the blissful hospitality of the bed.

In an analogical world that gave me birth, the measure of relationships is the analog of gestures.

The space of a phone call is a time sought and dedicated. Confined to the corner between receiver, wire, and handset.

My thought for you is a ring on the intercom. I was passing by here. You will never know if by chance or not. But you can ask. Then maybe I'll answer you, and it doesn't mean I'm lying.

The persistence of the sea and the heartbeats is marked by the physicality of a postman.

—Write to me—, —do we write to each other?—, it is expectation and hope, sometimes a lie.

The envelope and the sender.

The recipient, unique, sealed by the sealing wax of a name and an address written in pen.

A letter is a letter. Unique, not superimposable if not with other ones, at the bottom of the desk and the memory of the years.

And then.

My adolescence is welcomed by a revolution.

The digital.

Digital comes from the English—digit—, which comes from the Latin digitus, which means—finger—.

In digital, analog values are transformed into numbers, digits, values.

It is the communication of the represented. Of the symbol, of the short, of the—stands for—.

Of incomprehensibility and misunderstanding.

8:10 means I have to get up, or I'll miss the first hour.

The envelope is now tiny and bright. And flashes on a monitor. It is accompanied by a number, which is always too high compared to the compartments of the heart. Too many address errors, too many unwanted destinations.

The digital. The speed of an efficiency that is no longer—proportionate—, analog.

The disappearance of all proportions makes the distances enormous and improbable to cover.

Like starting over, the need to rewrite the minimal topography of an orientation.

Knowing where to go. And how to get there.

I do not know how much it is because it is no longer as much as it is. And more.

Everything to be rewritten.

An analogic heart in a digital world.

A beat that marks the times of a feeling—as much as—, in a world that is now—stands for—

What a rip-off.

In this world, there are only two tragedies:

One is not getting what one wants, and the second is

getting it.

[O. Wilde]

I must have read it in a book a few years ago.

To desire.

From the Latin—*de*— (lack, separation) and—*sider, sideris*— (stars).

Sometimes the etymology of a term is more explanatory than a thousand dissertations.

—Distance from the stars—.

That sidereal, mysterious, densely empty space that separates us from the stars.

And it is precisely in the distance that a desire is substantiated.

An unbridgeable distance that is the very essence of pushing me towards. Action and creation.

Thousand times sung, dedicated, dreamed. The stars, there.

And here, my gaze towards.

In the middle, a space of separation that is contemplation and motor.

Fertile emptiness, yearning.

I desire precisely because this is where I am.

Feet to the earth, look at the stars.

Chapter II
The Others and Me

People where you live grow five thousand roses in one garden, yet they don't find what they're looking for.

And yet what they're looking for could be found in a single rose or a little water.

But eyes are blind.

[Antoine de Saint-Exupéry, The Little Prince]

In the age of total communication and eyes down on cell phones, relationships work when they are made up of small, bright phrases.

Billions of words given away to a screen intertwine the threads of false ties that fall apart with reality.

And when we are face to face, we don't know each other again.

Because knowing each other is flesh, blood, smells, breath, looks, slowness, boredom, embarrassment, sighs, and hesitations.

Without it, it is too easy to fall into the deception of idealizations.

In the era of total communication, we desperately need to get back to really communicating, looking each other in the eye.

How to re-learn to be human. Flesh and spirit, dreams and reality.

What a paradox.

"Homo sum, humani nihil a me alienum puto"

I am a man; I do not think anything human is unknown to me.

[Terenzio Afro]

Each behavioral mode is a continuum that embraces opposite polarities.

Some are precise, some superficial.

Some are punctual, some latecomer.

Some are emotional, some detached.

Some are protective, some demanding.

Some are dependent, some individualistic.

The behavioral modalities are structured during the first years of life.

These are real—choices—often unconscious. The most adaptive solutions are taken by the child to survive emotionally and face difficult situations.

These are choices that then crystallize, determining ways of being in the world that, in adulthood, may be dysfunctional, obsolete, or in any case inadequate adaptations to the present situation. There cannot be a better adaptation that is universally valid, but the possibility and the ability to adapt, flexibly and adequately, to the situation experienced from time to time in the present.

Living on a single polarity means denying oneself the possibility of experiencing oneself in a different form, embracing new ways that may also be more suitable to today.

And we can choose to explore our—existential choices—, going back to the decisions and the original scenes that determined them, and the relative prohibitions received, to allow ourselves the opportunity to experience one's part left in the shade, regaining possession of potential, and sometimes surprising, energy source left unexplored.

Slowly dies whoever becomes a slave to habit,

repeating the same paths every day (...)

[M. Medeiros]

Oh no, don't believe it.

There is a difference between determination and stubbornness.

There is a difference between stubbornness and rigidity.

—That's the way I am—is the biggest devaluation you can amount to.

Changing the path is healthy.

Having doubts is healthy.

Experiencing a different form of self is healthy.

The fullness is in flexibility, not in rigid obstinacy.

It is the loss of the ability to adapt that leads to much suffering. Everything changes, evolves, and do you expect to always remain the same?

Stop. Be aware of your reflexes. Reassuring, of course, but certainly limiting.

There is so much of you there, in the shadows.

Welcome it, give it voice, enlighten it.

Discover yourself new, different, and the same.

And take back the fullness of who you are.

Before you heal someone,

ask him if he is willing to give up

to the things that made him sick.

Hippocrates wrote it about 2500 years ago.

Many forms of malaise and illness have psychic and emotional origins. In the literature, we speak of somatization: anxiety, headache, osteoarticular pain, gastric and intestinal disorders, sense of malaise, and fatigue.

Body and psyche are not two distinct entities but a single and inseparable entity in continuous interaction. Just think of stomachache before an exam, redness on the face when we are embarrassed, trepidation after a fright.

The psyche resides in the body and permeates it.

And so, burdensome and recurring moods inevitably end up being reflected in the body. Medicines treat the symptom and not the cause. They act on a biochemical level to eliminate pain or imbalance but, obviously, cannot work on the triggers. From this point of view, effective therapy is passing through awareness of the causes to stop expressing themselves through the body. Consciousness also requires an act of responsibility; to stop looking for reasons, faults, and solutions outside oneself and run the risk of changing one's way of being in the world. Live, following your values, free to Be and to decide.

Behind every illness

there is a ban on doing something we want

or the order to do something we do not want.

Each therapy requires disobedience to this prohibition or order. [A. Jodorowsky]

There is a disorder that cannot be related to any known diagnostic category. It does not show up from examinations or clinical tests of any kind, nor can it be found in the DSM (the reference text of psychiatric disorders).

Men and women suffer from it, often married, mothers of families, fathers.

It manifests itself with symptoms of various kinds. Muscle and bone pains, chronic fatigue, irregular breathing, weight on the chest, gastric and intestinal disorders; is a malaise that often changes shape and target organ.

Doctors don't get over it, often dismissing it as an—anxiety disorder—. But what is it really?

Often it is the body that screams the detachment from its self.

A messenger who warns us that we are not living according to our innermost values and desires.

A muffled scream (from society, from family, from what is right or wrong, from feelings of guilt, from—what must be done—), that reminds us that we are taking the wrong path,

that the only way is the one that leads to the center of oneself,

that there is always time, you just need to want it,

it's time to stop being afraid,

that the comfort zone is sometimes a golden cage,

and that—too late—is only authentic when the heart has beaten its last beat.

Courage; from the Latin *cor, cordis*, —heart—, and *habere*, —to have—.

Literally —to have heart—.

And as long as that heart beats, a choice is always possible.

Beginning: [from Latin principium, der. of princeps -cĭpis in the meaning of —first—].

Beginning, the act, and the fact of starting.

It's a matter of principle.

I heard that many times.

But a principle is something that guides and nurtures. The foundations of growth, the sprout of a beginning.

Too many matters of principle, granitic, obtuse, and irreducible, are instead matters of the end of relationships and growth.

We complain profusely,

but we become cowards

when it comes to taking action.

We want everything to change,

but we refuse to change ourselves.

[Paulo Coelho, Like the Flowing River, 2006]

I tell you something that may seem trivial to you.

As long as you attribute the cause of your complaints outside yourself, nothing can change.

No one on this planet has ever been powerful enough to change anyone. Only those who want to change can do it. And sometimes complaining is just the easiest way to avoid taking action.

But if you are willing to look within, then you will understand that much of your pain you are choosing.

Maybe with a non-choice.

Just as you always choose your emotions.

Don't say—you make me angry—, but—I choose to be angry—.

The reappropriation of the origin and responsibility of your emotions allows you to rediscover a power that is sometimes deliberately forgotten, the possibility to decide, always.

> So, what do you choose today?
> *You can't make the same mistake twice.*
> *The second time you do it*
> *it is no longer an error, but a choice*

I don't know whose quote is, but I've seen it frequently on Facebook lately.

It receives a lot of feedback and likes because many identify with it.

Who among us has not found himself complaining/saying that he found himself in the same situation as some time before almost automatically (and unconsciously)?

Some regularly find themselves in situations that clash with failure. Some find themselves being a mistress. Some embark on unrealistic stories. Some never find work outside their city. Some always end up being a victim of others. Some are punctually betrayed, disappointed, overwhelmed.

Perhaps the quotation is not correct. A conscious choice, in fact, presupposes the total freedom of conditioning and pre-structuring.

There is me, the reality of things, my evaluation of events, and my ability and freedom to choose the solution that I consider best.

But it is an ideal and proto-typical situation that rarely corresponds to the reality of our existences.

Eric Berne, the founder of the therapeutic approach known as Transactional Analysis, speaks of a—life script—, defining it as a pre-programmed plan (a sort of script, score) based on cognitive, emotional, or behavioral decisions made in childhood on about oneself, about others and the world. These decisions guide life and limit autonomy, awareness, and the ability to be intimate and flexible in various forms.

Therapy helps to identify these automatic ways that push people to repetitive and rigid behaviors, often totally inadequate to the present situation.

Understanding its origin and structure allows the person to redecide on his own existence and fully regain possession of his freedom to choose the most suitable way of being in the world.

So yes, the first can be a mistake; the second an authentic choice.

> *Men at some time are masters of their fates.*
>
> *The fault, dear Brutus, is not in our stars,*
>
> *but in ourselves, that we are underlings.*
>
> *[Shakespeare, Cassius: act I, scene II]*

A difficult childhood, the lack of affection, an unfortunate fate, the mother, the father, a relationship that ended badly, a disappointment, a betrayal, a loss.

—Here, this is why I am like this—, —It is its fault—.

The person's character takes form during the first six/seven years of life based on the first experiences of attachment (his parents, or whoever for him) and the first live events. During childhood, the child in a more or less unconscious form establishes what in Transactional Analysis are defined as— script decisions—.

—Since ... then I'll be in the world like this—.

The awareness of one's history allows one to understand one's automatisms (in behavior, decisions, choices, relational modalities) and rediscover one's freedom of action.

Choose a path, this time different.

There is a moment in a person's life (and in therapy) where the individual must take back their responsibility and freedom of action. It is no longer the fault of an inauspicious ate, of parents, of others. It's a choice, my choice. This road, or another. Difficult, tiring, but possible and independent.

Geometries of Existence

The infinity in mathematics has the form of an inverted 8.

Like the tracks of some little trains, we built as children.

But how much freedom is there in a short circuit that always repeats the same path?

Errare humanum est, persevere autem diabolicum.

To err is human, to persevere ... also.

We often complain when we find ourselves in life situations that have the character of déjà-vu, of the already seen, already experienced.

It is essential to become aware of this. It is not always an ominous coincidence.

Freud called it—the compulsion to repeat—. He defines it as the unconscious tendency of the individual to re-propose situations, even painful and dysfunctional, a sort of—psychic redemption—, second (third, fourth, fifth ...) possibility.

It is the inevitable, sometimes frustrating, feeling of finding oneself in life contexts (relationships, choices, situations) repeated in our personal history.

Some paths must be taken, open gestalts (forms) that ask to be closed. Like a jammed turntable, it always repeats the same turn, the same score. The same —already heard—, until a hand, now saturated and tired, chooses to re-channel the needle towards its melodic flow.

So we too can redecide.

Our scripts, our repetition, our choices, and relationships.

To free oneself from that 8, from a closed and mortifying short circuit, to embrace new, and fuller, existential possibilities of being in the world.

Now yes, finally free.

If I have good feelings,

I will find good feelings in the world too.

Every virtue that I make reality

belongs to the human species.

If you turn on the lamp of beauty,

There will be beauty in the world.

When a flower blooms,

Spring is everywhere.

[A. Jodorowsky, The answer is the question]

Have you ever wondered why areas of degradation exist and persist? (city districts, dysfunctional families, political environments, workplaces, etc.).

The lack of resources, the economic hardship, only partially explain the persistence of what, at a certain point, becomes an atmosphere, a hood, something detached, autonomous, as though with a life of its own; no longer an effect but also a cause, in a self-reinforcing and deadly circuit.

The theory of—broken windows—(an interesting sociological idea born from an experiment in America) demonstrates how, in high structural degradation environments, individuals feel as if they are—authorized— to take part in equally degrading acts and gestures.

If I live in a dirty city, I will tend to dirty it.

If I live in a violent family, violence can also be my language.

But if degradation can spread like a disease, so can beauty.

Good calls good, beauty calls beauty, light calls light.

—Okay, but I'm alone, and what can I do?—. It's just a discouraging excuse not to start.

Everything starts with something or someone.

Every idea, every work, every journey, every business.

And then that gesture expands, like the warmth of a fireplace or the scent of coffee in a house.

So let's let that first flower emerge from a frosty winter scenario.

Light calls the light, and soon it will be spring.

We are all taught to be cultured,

not to be innocent

or to perceive the wonder of existence.

We are taught the names of flowers; some trees

and not how to communicate with them,

in tune with existence.

Existence is a mystery and is not accessible

to those who always want to analyze, select,

but only to those who are willing to fall in love with it,

to dance with it."

[Acharya Osho Rajneesh]

Fritz Perls, the founder of Gestalt therapy, called it—the eidetic child—. It is the condition of the very young child who, for the first time in front of a rose, widens his eyes and exclaims—ooooh!—.

It is the direct and immediate experience of pure feeling.

Subsequently, the parents, faced with that pure—feeling—, intervene by attributing a name to that amazement—look, it's a rose!—. And this is how they open the way to an experience that is no longer immediate and pure but mediated by a name and subject to evaluation.

The rose is now no longer that ooooh! And that feeling, but it is a rose, and it can be red, yellow, big, small, beautiful, ugly.

This is how a linguistic code, fundamental and indispensable for sharing and communication within a social and cultural system, creates a classification of superstructures that filters and, inevitably, modifies the original experience.

There is a profound difference between explaining and feeling. And wanting to explain everything is often a trap that leads away from the genuine experience.

Existence is a mystery, says Osho, and so much of what belongs to it is not one way or another, but simply—is—.

Learning to feel, to—be—truly and fully in the experience, to—fall in love with it—without judgment, opens the way to a fuller, centered, and profound existence.

"It is not the strongest of the species that survives,

nor the most intelligent,

it is the one most adaptable to change"

[Charles Darwin]

Changing is vital and often very difficult.

Mankind's existence is characterized by impermanence. — Panta Rei— wrote Heraclitus, —everything flows—.

Everything is in motion, changes.

There is nothing, living being or phenomenon, in our world that is not in constant evolution.

Bodies change, relationships change, seasons, things, landscapes change. Statuses change, homes, jobs, hobbies, tastes, clothes, situations change.

But the ways of reacting, relating, thinking, living, and feeling often struggle to adapt to changes.

In Transactional Analysis, the—script decisions—(the best possible form of adaptation developed during childhood) tend to stiffen and emerge, today, in situations, times, places, no longer responding to the need at that time. These are characteristic habits that risk strongly limiting the individual's freedom and ability to react in a responsible and adult way to the plurality of situations that arise.

It is a bit like wanting to compose a melody using always the same and few notes.

Psychic suffering arises from this lack of flexibility in adapting to a constantly changing world. You get attached to everything; relationships, memories, work, people who are no longer there, old loves, back in the days. Thus sacrificing the only and fundamental certainty of our being in the world: the here and now, this moment. The present.

Free will is one of the philosophical themes that has always sparked discussions and reflections among scientists and thinkers of all time; is a human being really free? Or is the much sought-after and vaunted freedom actually a pure illusion? Perhaps we cannot speak of true freedom when so many of us work with more or less unconscious automatisms and legacies. But the freedom to choose, act, and be can be won every day. With the awareness of our history, automatisms, of the numerous and sometimes heavy psychic residues that we carry with us from ancient times.

Knowing each other to really be.

Panta rei, everything flows.

We decide whether to flow with or flow against.

What Would Cinderella Be Like Today?

"...and they lived happily ever after"

In Transactional Analysis, the Life Script is described as a protocol (almost a score) established on early childhood decisions concerning parental injunctions (messages).

The life script makes the existence of an individual inflexible, sometimes predictable. It is to find oneself, in a more or less unconscious form, always in similar situations (same type of partner, the same work situation, the same family dynamic), a sort of—a compulsion to repeat—. In Freud's words, it pushes the individual to a perennial repetition, in the desire (at most destined to fail), to finally close an ancient, open, unresolved gestalt (form, configuration).

Who knows what Cinderella would be like today.

If she is true to her script, maybe she would be busy with the housework. In a different scenario, of course. A castle; much more rooms to clean.

But still busy, oppressed, and dissatisfied.

Alone in a castle, and the prince who knows where probably to—save—new girls.

The truth is, it is not princes that save.

Nobody has this power. We save ourselves with our own strength and the deep desire to change.

Through a profound work on ourselves to identify our dysfunctional patterns and modalities, and redecide our existence in the direction of true and total freedom of being.

And she lived, today, free and full.

It's Now or Never

Chapter III

A Sense Beyond the Senses

What we did not dare,

we have certainly lost.

(Oscar Wilde)

Thought is the highest and most complex form of the human being, the outcome of millions of years of evolution.

But even such a complex tool can turn into a cage.

No thought will ensure you the—right choice—. None will keep you from making mistakes.

The human is also the oldest part of him, the amygdala, a brain area deriving directly from the reptilian brain.

Instinct, intuition, action is indispensable and often devalued components of human nature.

And, if you try and fail, you learn something. Always.

It is said that Edison made thousands of attempts to improve the invention of the light bulb (approximately 2,000). During a press conference, a reporter asked him, "Mr. Edison, how did it feel to fail two thousand times in making a light bulb?"

Edison's response was,

"I haven't failed two thousand times to make a light bulb. I simply found 1999 ways of how not to do it."

No thought alone will lead you to a real discovery.

Fritz Perls, the founder of gestalt therapy, also said so.

Experiment, dare, try.

And only then will you know.

The most important day of your life is when you understand that the life you are living is—whether you like it or not—the only one you have.

It is certainly not infinite.

Sure, you have time.

To grow and believe in it, to change direction,

to make a bunch of mistakes,

to cry and get excited,

to really meet others,

to discover the unknown world,

to choose another path,

to try again.

You have time. But it is certainly not infinite.

So what's the point of still being angry?

Why complain, blame others, mull over old wounds?

The life you live is the only one you have.

And maybe you can choose, today, to start loving it, feeling it, giving it the value it deserves.

And if that's not the life you want, then move on and start changing it.

There is no life without risks to run.

And no right or wrong is for everyone.

The right thing is the one you feel by listening to your heart.

Happiness is love, nothing else.

Happy is he who knows how to love.

Love is every movement of our soul in which

it feels itself and perceives its own life.

[Hermann Hesse]

But, after all, what is happiness?

It is not the absence of pain. That is a utopia. An ideal. Unrealizable, detached from reality, immobile.

Life is an alternation of states. It is impermanence. It is a pain, smile, tears, hesitation, conquests, love, disappointments, courage, fears, discovery, loss, amazement.

Happiness is, therefore, fullness. It is freedom, awareness.

It is laughing with all your smile and crying with all your tears.

Come away, O human child!

To the waters and the wild

With a fairy, hand in hand.

For the world's more full of weeping

than you can understand.

[W. B. Yeats]

Never cease to be amazed,

to seek the magic in the ordinary,

to see the new in the known,

to move your foot on the first step,

to wait for the dawn from the depths of the darkest days,

to smile at this Now,

to your beating heart.

And fall asleep on a new desire, let go of what has been,

unfold the sails to new landings and new smiles.

I carry the wounds of all the battles I have avoided.

[F. Pessoa]

There are unspoken phrases, unspoken gestures, closed eyes in rooms of pain.

Out of fear, out of pain, out of resignation, out of neglect.

A silent, invisible, underground magma. Seemingly harmless.

Which then suddenly brings out her voice.

It makes itself felt.

Unspoken sentences want to be spoken.

Suspended gestures want to be done.

Closed eyes want to open up, look into those rooms that have been kept too long in the dark.

Letting the pain flow, looking at it, living it, feeling it means allowing the doors to close and the wounds to heal.

Courage

Courage: etymology derived from the Latin *cor, cordis,* —heart— and from the verb *habere,* —to have—. Literally—I have a heart—.

Courage is not something you have or don't have.

This thought is often the excuse for not trying, for not taking risks.

Courage is something you can choose to bring out.

Because it is in you, inherent in your heartbeat, in your throbbing.

For the sole fact of being alive.

Emotions

"If someone approaches you with a gift and you don't accept it, who does the gift belong to?" asked the samurai. "To those who tried to give it away", replied one of the disciples.

"The same goes for envy, anger, and insults", said the master. "When they are not accepted, they continue to belong to those who brought them with them."

[Zen anecdote]

There are no positive and negative emotions.

Emotions are all functional and indispensable.

—Inside Out—the new animated film from Pixar, has highlighted, simply and visually, the fundamental role of sadness as an essential element not only to enter into empathic resonance with others but also to look inside and feel deep down a dissatisfaction or the need for change.

And the same goes for fear which has allowed us to survive and evolve by recognizing potentially dangerous situations.

Anger also has its social and adaptive function. It allows you to establish social boundaries, a clear message to avoid dysfunctional territorial invasions or offenses to one's person.

No emotion is in itself pathological or—negative—. All are indispensable and vital; emotions tend, in fact, towards the adaptation and survival of the individual.

Negative is the crystallization of emotion, its persistence beyond the field of direct functionality, and its decontextualization beyond the—here and now—of its manifestation. It is like being afraid when there is no real danger, or still being angry about something long gone.

Negative is also the lack of recognition or the lack of expression of the natural emotion and its replacement with another one, parasitic. For example, sadness is often replaced with anger, an emotion perceived as more—active—and therefore more pleasant for those who experience and maintain it.

And so, we can still be angry with that partner who left us or with that person who committed a wrong against us years ago. One can still be angry with a parent for their errors, or with oneself (but anger retroflexed on oneself is unnatural, dysfunctional, and destructive) for choices or behaviors that are today the cause of repentance.

And the most common justification for the persistence of this emotion is—he deserves it, I *can't* forgive him—. As if *one's* anger were to wrong the existence of *others*, magically re-establishing an ancient imbalance.

But a persevered emotion is something strictly personal. It remains trapped in the psychic structure of those who live and maintain it. The other is perhaps now concretely out of its direct range of application.

Therefore, keeping it takes away something from oneself; energy, serenity, and smile, in a spiral of self-torment of which one is both the creators and victims.

Today it is only ours the *choice* to be angry or to forgive, to kick or accept. An act of grace and respect no longer towards the other but towards one's own life and well-being.

> *Forgive others*
>
> *not because they deserve forgiveness*
>
> *but because you deserve peace.*
>
> *[ancient Chinese proverb]*

Amusement

From the Latin devèrtere: formed by—*de*—(which indicates distancing) and by—*vèrtere*—(which means to turn).

Literally—turning elsewhere—in the opposite direction.

Fun as the possibility of deviating from a usual direction.

It is soothing to want to always feel the same. There is no risk or gasp. A calm and comfortable certainty. Like the toll of midnight, the softness of the head on the pillow, the warmth of a blanket, the smell of coffee in the morning.

But always wanting the same is like living halfway. A half that gives security, but still a half.

We are made of polarity. And on the many steps of this ladder, settling on the same rung means denying yourself something.

The possibility of being amazed.

To wonder.

Like rain on the beach on a summer day, northern lights in the middle of the night, a flower that rises between the tracks of an old station.

The Strength of Weakness

To be perfect, one lacks only a defect.
[Karl Kraus]

True greatness is not in being perfect or strong.

True greatness is in being genuine and intimate, with oneself and with others.

The points of fragility, often hidden, eclipsed, relegated to their own shaded areas, are the same that bring people closer.

Authentic points of contact between souls.

Each mask takes us away from our true essence.

No one is all good, all true, all strong, all fragile.

Growth is never in the abandonment of parts of oneself, in oblivion, but the conscious reappropriation of one's own contrasts and polarities.

Happiness, Nothing Else

Almost anonymous, you smile

and the sky gilds your hair.

Because to be happy,

is it necessary not to know?

[Fernando Pessoa]

Happiness is a process, not a goal.

Nobody can—get to be happy—. As if it were a place, a podium, the top of a mountain.

Because the worst risk that can be run in the frantic conquest of happiness is to lose it.

Happiness is an intrinsic quality of the human being. Something so intimate and personal. Like sadness, melancholy, or any other emotion.

We do not find it on the street or in objects.

It is not provided by our partner or our parents.

We can discover happiness in us, in our everyday life, in the authenticity of our most profound being.

Happiness is a state of fullness of one's being and one's feeling.

It is a state of awareness, free from conditionings and blocks that affect our free flow.

It is to immerse yourself fully and confidently among the sinuous waves of life, fully experiencing all it offers.

A treasure, sometimes hidden, but which is deep in each of us. And that once identified and accepted, no one can ever take us away.

This is the way to liberation.

To You, Woman

You deserve a love that wants you disheveled,

with everything and all the reasons that wake you up in haste, with everything and the demons that won't let you sleep.

You deserve a love that makes you feel secure, able to take on the world when it walks behind you,

that feels your embraces are perfect for its skin.

You deserve a love that wants to dance with you,

that goes to paradise every time it looks into your eyes

and never gets tired of studying your expressions.

You deserve a love that listens when you sing, that supports you when you act like a fool that respects your freedom;

that accompanies you when you fly and isn't afraid to fall.

You deserve a love that takes away the lies and brings you illusion, coffee, and poetry.

[Frida Kahlo]

You were born disheveled, and you can look at yourself and like yourself.

With that tenderness that embraces your gaze, pure and resting on your face.

Everything is a set of things, is the wholeness of your being, something that belongs to you and that no one can give you or take away from you.

And yes, if you really look, you will always find a reason to get up and say hello to a new day.

Fears and doubts, even those belonging to you. We are human, and darkness will always be the other part of the day. But like the night, it passes if you know how to wait and accept even the grim and the silence.

Security is home and mountains, the center of you that remains immutable despite everything flowing around, always. But remember, life is also made up of little follies. And then, there is also the risk that insecurity can be the basis for a new balance.

Learn to taste what you eat, to nourish yourself with smells, sensations, and images. The world is full of beauty, and you can feel it resonate in your senses. You are made of the same stuff.

Dance when and with whoever you want. Alone, in the company. The other may choose to follow your steps in synchrony that will be magic and enchantment. And, when the music ends, learn to say hello, by thanking you for that moment of wonder. You have your legs, and a new melody is already in the air if you can listen to it.

Get lost, to find yourself every time. Let dreams be the engine of your days. Heaven is here on this earth. Look others in the eyes when you meet them.

In their eyes, and not yours, you can really see them.

Move, let your body follow your feelings freely. Leave the protocols in the offices and armies.

Use your voice. To express, to sing. But also learn to stop. Maybe there is another melody in the air, and listening to it will enrich you.

It is ridiculous not to move, not to try. We are all imperfect, and therefore wonderful and unique.

You were born free. Discover, travel, touch, get dirty with the smells and flavors of the world. Use your body without limits or guilt.

Fly to the heights and for as long as you want. And remember that taking the leap means accepting the fear of falling. You will stumble, but you will rise stronger with new wings and new goals to reach. Only those who want to stop will stop.

Be honest with yourself before others. Accept limits and gray areas. Nothing is all white or all black. Fifty Shades of Gray aren't just in novels.

Dream. Your dreams are your creatures. Nobody can take them off or give them to you. They are yours, always and in any case.

Open your eyes and breathe. It's already morning. The smell of coffee means home.

Wherever you are, may the scent of every morning be always new to you.

It's a new day, and poetry is already in the air and your gestures.

Stop.

Breathe.

Live this moment, it's all you have.

Because there is no ONE world.

The world exists as I perceive it and choose to live it.

Snow can be a nuisance for some and magic for others.

Rain can be damnation or blessing.

The night can be either refreshment or fear.

And then I take back all power.

If it depends on me, then I'll be the one who wants it.

It is my world, and I will make light and beauty be in me.

Love

Love doesn't have to beg or even demand,

love must have the strength to become certainty within

itself.

[H. Hesse]

Expectations sometimes screw you.

And they become the seed of widespread, creeping, persistent unhappiness, which in the long run can wear down the couple's relationships.

Expect your partner to say or do something without even voicing your needs and taking responsibility for asking and speaking.

As if stating them in some way debased them or mortified the relationship.

Expecting without asking is a characteristic of the child's ego state.

A very young child does not have the tools to ask.

Mothers are extraordinarily good at understanding the needs of their little ones and coping with them, converting into actions and words an undifferentiated push that cannot have a voice.

But adult love is different.

Adult love passes through the ability to ask, communicate, and make oneself known.

Without pretensions or magical expectations but with the courage to be oneself with the other.

I, You, and a shared and open space that becomes the fertile ground for the—we—.

The belief that one's own view of reality is the only reality is the most dangerous of all delusions.

[P. Watzlawick, How real is real]

Yes, I Confess

One of the main reasons that lead to innumerable misunderstandings, couple conflicts, irremediable generational gaps, frustrations, and disappointments is the same that lead to mutual enrichment and a real meeting; our profound diversity.

Each of us is the result of an unrepeatable blend of genetic factors and environmental experiences.

Unique.

Each of us is his own story, his parents, the house he lived in, his brothers/sisters or their absence, his losses, his defeats, his talents, his teachings and understandings, his rebellions, his refusals, his loves, his deep values, his senses, his discoveries, his desires.

We know this well, yet we continue to live, perceive, want, and desire (if not expect) the other through our parameters of evaluation and judgment.

What it—should—do. The way it—should—be. What —should be—right.

But right for who?

Ending, in the most extreme cases, not to see the other at all, or rather not really wanting to see him, and to accept him for what he is.

Decentralizing to really meet (and understand) the other and his world is a gesture of deep and mature love.

Everything else is ego, fear, and pride. We don't realize the boundaries of our being limit us to a unique and limited reality that imprisons us, denying us the encounter with the possibility of looking outside us.

And get a little more, and a little richer.

Before judging my life or my character

put on my shoes, walk the path I walked.

Experience my pain, my doubts, my laughter.

Live the years that I have lived

and fall where I fell and stand up like I did.

[Luigi Pirandello]

Love me still now

I'm always Luca, the same.

["Luca lo stesso", Luca Carboni, 2015]

In a world where everything is impermanent, people change too. And often, love relationships are affected. The inflexibility to change or the (un) conscious—forgetfulness— cause tensions and ruptures.

Umberto Galimberti, in his essay—The Things of Love—, describes this delicate passage from a psychoanalytic point of view.

It is the (natural and functional) effect of the degradation process to which we submit relationships to guarantee the passage from the risk and ecstasy of falling in love with the need for security and stability necessary for the construction of the concepts of—home— and—family—.

In short, we trade happiness for security.

But what is paradoxical is that this very process slowly builds and nourishes the ground for our dissatisfactions and escapes.

And so, as in so many human issues, we end up as victims and perpetrators of our miseries.

—The other— has to do with it only in part, taken in a two-way game of continuous readjustments in a self-perpetuating circle of which cause and effect are lost.

And then, perhaps, before accusing and complaining, it is better to stop and reflect.

What are we doing to bring about the slow decay of our relationship day after day?

Have we perhaps stopped really seeing the other, deforming his being to a stereotyped form that mortifies his essence?

Maybe you pretend you don't know. Or stop remembering it. Yet, that man on the sofa who is your husband today is the same person who years ago ran with you on a motorcycle to discover unknown worlds full of poetry and beauty.

And yet, that woman today worn out by her rhythms is the same one you loved on a beach lit by the moon and the shivers of your excitement.

—Everything must change so that everything remains the same—wrote Giuseppe Tomasi di Lampedusa.

Getting to know each other cannot be a reductive process.

Like searching for fundamental functional elements in a perfect and predictable mathematical system.

Here we are talking about people.

Blood, flesh, and intellect inseparably intertwine with a spiritual, elusive, and unpredictable—something—. And perhaps even unknowable.

It is not true that you perfectly know who is by your side.

This is just an alibi you provide yourself to meet *your* need for security and predictability.

But, in doing so, you mortify and devalue the other and his most vital, poetic, electrifying, and alive part.

And then maybe you say—you are not the same anymore, you changed—.

And you are disappointed.

And run away.

We are people. Beautiful and imperfect. Full of lights, shadows, mystery, and poetry.

"Two boys who love each other

and who knows if we are still so stupid.

Love me still now

I'm always Luca, the same."

["Luca lo stesso", Luca Carboni]

The Half of Two

You are you

and I am I.

I am not in this world to live up to your expectations,

and you are not in this world to live up to mine.

And if by chance we find each other, it's beautiful

If not, it can't be helped.

[Fritz Perls]

In the Symposium, Plato narrated through the intervention of Aristophanes a myth. Once upon a time, men were beings with four arms, four legs, two heads, and both sexual organs, male and female. They were skilled, fast, and perfect beings, capable of self-reproduction.

Zeus, worried about their power and abilities, decided to punish them by dividing them into two parts; two halves, condemned to wander the world for the complementary other (the—missing half—) to regain lost unity and completeness.

Love is not the meeting of two halves but two units.

Many forms of emotional dependence find their basis in the perception of oneself as incomplete, imperfect, —empty— that the other can and must fill.

Hence the tendency to seek in the other the closure of an incomplete Gestalt (form), which often finds its roots in the very first bonds of attachment.

"Women Who Love Too Much," by R. Norwood, an American psychologist, was an editorial bestseller. It collects stories of women united by couple relationships based on themes of addiction and oppression.

Women who love the other too much or women who love themselves too little?

Christ also said—Love your neighbor (but) as you love yourself.

So, self-love not as a presupposition that borders on individualism but as the founding basis of the capacity for love for the other.

Just so love can be an encounter between two units, a genuine, equal exchange, based on sharing and not on projections, expectations, lethal devaluation, and oppression.

"Two is not double but the opposite of one, of its loneliness. Two is an alliance, a double thread that is not broken." (Erri de Luca)

Two. The couple. The opposite of one, not half.

Separation is the prerequisite for all recognition.

—I am me, you are you—, said F. Perls.

And it is precisely in the acceptance of the other as—other than oneself—that the possibility of a real encounter is substantiated.

Wanting the other in the image of one's desires is simply not desiring the other.

It is necessary to re-know oneself before being able to meet.

"My love for you ends when I limit your freedom, your Essence, your Being...

There can be no Love without the freedom to be oneself." (E. Fromm)

"Volo ut sis", St. Augustine used to say about love.

—I want you to be who you are—without trying to change you and without trying to change me to please you.

I love you for who you are, just as you are.

Everything else is only mortifying control, overwhelm, fear.

These have very little to do with love, which must remain a choice of freedom, growth, acceptance, and profound respect.

"I Love You"

What does this sentence contain?

What am I loving when I say it?

We often confuse love with the emotions we experience concerning the other.

Something positive, or negative, activated by the presence (or absence) of the partner.

But emotions are something personal, ours. It is like saying that we love a part of ourselves that is activated with the presence of the one we say we love.

In short, all very self-centered.

But love is something else.

—I love YOU—contains within itself that—you—, only three letters that build bridges of extraordinary strength.

They are interconnection, gateway, and encounter.

It is the act of—going out of oneself—to meet the other.

To love someone is to want the best for *him*, even if it meant letting them go.

How often do we get angry because the other person does not act, live, feel, and behave as we expect?

A bit like saying—at this moment, you have not met my expectations—. But expectations arise from *our* images.

Creations of desires, empty spaces, conflicts, and dynamics that belong to us and that we project onto the other.

But the other is certainly not responsible for it. Yet we attribute weight and a compensatory role to the partner, heavy baggage that certainly does not belong to him.

The other is, in fact, *another person*.

Another story, other dynamics, voids, desires, and conflicts.

Love is respect; from the Latin *respicere*, composed of *re-spicere*, —to look again—.

Love is having care and consideration for the other.

Some things require the delicacy of gentle touch, and another person's life is definitely one of them.

The Web of Feelings

Everyone seems to want something far away.

Or they want someone who wants someone else.

Desires are lost yearnings.

They chase each other, they rarely meet.

Tracing them on an imaginary sheet of paper, they compose a spider's web with neurotic and imperfect symmetries.

Straight lines, sometimes a breath away.

In the chaos of overlaps and chases, they happen to meet. It is in that rare miracle that a knot is born.

That is an important point. It holds the entire structure.

You can tighten a knot. And it is the magic of encounter that gives solidity to the entire canvas.

Or you can melt it. Untying the strings from the prison of disasters.

Free, to chase the wind.

Distances

The world, seen from above, loses disorder.

There are distances to get lost.

Minimal distances made of smells and sighs.

Extreme distances, where to not lose the thread is suspended between courage and recklessness.

Apparent distances, distant distances, distances of rooms.

And then the right ones, the correct distances; the silent discovery of belonging, of a sense beyond the senses.

The hidden thread that intertwines everything.

The petal is from the flower, the leaf is from the forest, the print is from the step on the path.

The Courage to Go

How much consistency does memory have in the present? No cell in your body is the same as when you were a child. None.

Your body is new. The persistence of infantile suffering or lack is a purely psychic question. A persistence that has the consistency of a nerve impulse in the shape of memory. Nothing of you today belongs to that child, no matter how much that child suffered.

Today you are an adult.

And, after anger and pain, it is sometimes necessary to let go of something to re-feel the weight of one's steps.

The present, your legs, and a road. Yours.

May your turning back be a look of thanks and understanding. It was what it could have been, in the form it could have been.

Today you are an adult.

The present, your legs, a road.

And the courage to go.

The pieces of glass scattered on the ground

come close again

go up the air

and on the shelf

a glass reappears

[N. Fabi, Ecco]

Take care of what is irreversible.

Take care of what is fragile and precious.

Take care of your desires, values, aspirations.

Take care of your innocence, your amazement, your excited gazes on the world. Take care of who you love and what you believe in. Take care of the moments, of your time, of your legs that whisper—go!—, and of your breath that reminds you every moment that you are alive.

Take care of it. Because not everything is circular, and not everything comes back.

Separation and Loss

"Like birds, after meeting

on the tree that hosts them, separate,

thus the meeting of creatures

it always ends with separation.

And like the clouds gather

and again they go away,

so I guess

it is the union and separation of living beings.

[Aśvaghoṣa]

Separation and loss are rather recurrent themes in psychotherapy.

The Neapolitan writer Erri De Luca in Aceto Arcobaleno (2002) writes—an opportune leave leaves behind a door that is always open—. But in cases of loss suffered and not chosen (grief or the end of a love story) what often happens is exactly the opposite; an inappropriate or non-existent leave leaves relational wakes and missed closures that can compromise the relational and affective serenity of the individual.

In psychotherapy, we speak of—grief processing—, a subject on which there is vast literature, also online for those interested in superior knowledge of the topic.

A loss, to be overcome, must be worked through.

The elaboration passes through several phases; from the — greeting—, to the—closing— of the unfinished business and the putting into words the unspoken, to the gratitude.

Finally, to arrive at the complete and conscious integration of the experience of—union— with the other in one's personal existence.

A presence no longer angry, painful, and restless but integrated, peaceful, enriching, and complete.

It is a backward journey, a slow retrace of your footsteps giving them a name, emotion, and voice.

Until the complete understanding that the loss of the other does not mean the loss of parts of oneself, since those parts have always been, and still are, in themselves and not in the other.

"The appearance of things varies according to emotions,

and so we see magic and beauty in them:

but beauty and magic are, in fact, in us."

[Kahlil Gibran, The broken wings]

Often the reaction to grief or the end of a love relationship is the disarming discouragement of not being able to relive the magic and the precious alchemy of the moments spent with those who are no longer there.

In the experience of falling in love, the person sees the world with other eyes and feels such inner strength to take risks that generally he does not dare to commit.

The mistake is to tie this view of the world and life and the growing perceived life force to the other.

The loss of the relationship then becomes the loss of one's life force.

But the reality is quite different. The alchemical magic and the life force are consequences of the connection with oneself that the person has lived in the love story.

The wonders experienced are the occurrence of one's soul and one's qualities, talents, and characteristics.

It is essential to realize that all the precious qualities experienced with the other (and activated by his encounter) actually belong to ourselves.

They are our little treasure.

And no one, by leaving, can take them away.

What must eventually contract,

at first, it must expand.

What must eventually weaken,

in the beginning, has to be strong.

What must ultimately be discarded,

in the beginning, must be embraced.

What must eventually be achieved,

in the beginning, it must be given.

[Lao Tzu]

A pain, a lack, a loss, a traumatic experience, a dissatisfaction.

Everything that presses to leave must first be welcomed and fully experienced to truly let go.

The strategy of—not seeing to not feeling—doesn't hold up after a while. It can't. The body knows. Feels. Communicates. Suffers. Even when we turn our eyes to ignore it.

As R. Frost said, the best way to solve a problem is to go through it.

All the way.

"You Disappointed Me"

How many times have we said or heard it? And then ferocious feelings of guilt started.

Can you disappoint someone by being *yourself*? A *self* that is much more varied, unpredictable, heterogeneous, and testy than the reassuring and simplified representation that we love to make of others and that others love to make of us.

Everyone is responsible for their own expectations or psychic constructions.

Don't say—you disappointed me—. Learn to really look at me for who I am.

Me, and not what you expect from me.

That's your stuff. It doesn't belong to me.

"You Abandoned Me"

How many psychic implications does a simple sentence contain that we pronounce to others or to ourselves?

Abandoning derives from the medieval French — *Abandonner*—, —*a bann donner*—, from *donn*, —power—, that is—to leave in power, at the mercy—.

It is a linguistic form that holds within itself a difference in power. Me, unable to face the world alone.

It can be well for a small child or a pet.

Not for me.

I have everything I need to go on and start over, and I will do it without you, with my strength.

You have not abandoned me. You have chosen another path, and I will follow mine.

You have not abandoned me.

You—gave me back to myself—.

And I decided to keep myself instead of letting go.

So I take my power back.

I stop blaming others for my unhappiness.

Except in rare cases, I am a victim only as long as I choose it.

So, I choose.

I take back my power.

And I transform this energy that I feel. No more anger that consumes me, but the lively desire to walk the road towards my smile.

You have nothing to do with it. Now it's just me.

"I Want to Be Happy"

It is time to abandon the myth of happiness as a promised land, a popular destination, a pleasant place to reach.

Happiness is not found. It is experienced. It is a natural state, inherent in our human being; no one and nothing can— introduce it into us—.

Let's get it in our heads; being happy is our only thing.

Ours is the responsibility of our unhappiness; we are very skilled in building tortuous labyrinths of situations or thoughts that distance us from that state of fullness and naturalness that can be defined as—feeling good—.

Observe the children; happiness is natural for them. We all have been, before allowing the ramblings of our thoughts to build our cages of unhappiness.

We choose ourselves, our path.

Let go of what is now outside our Now.

Let's rediscover the simplicity of Being.

Let's think about today and not about tomorrow.

And the happiness, so long sought, will soon blossom. Thus, naturally.

Like a seed becomes a flower, and a ray of serenity pierces the clouds after a storm.

Nostalgia

Fall in love with days of love

Maybe not even lived

In the memory transfigured in the sun.

[E. Ruggeri, Il primo amore non si scorda mai]

The Greek word for—return— is *nòstos. Álgos* means — suffering—. Nostalgia is, therefore, the suffering caused by the unfulfilled desire to return (from Ignorance, M. Kundera).

The idealization of the past is one of the best ways to make oneself unhappy (P. Watzlawick).

Yes.

We were younger, more carefree, happier. We were more.

—How beautiful is youth—.

Yet we will remember well that even then, there were anxieties, disappointments, pains, waits.

Maybe something was missing.

But, due to a curious mechanism in our psyche, we forget it. And the result is what is called idealization.

A detachment of something or someone from the ground of objectivity.

Maybe then we thought we would be happy when we got a driver's license or a job, a house of our own, or children.

We idealized the future.

And then it all came. And now?

What pays the price is our present, our now, the only load of real potential, mortified and diluted by an overwhelming and nostalgic past or by an expected and hoped future that takes away its flavor, color, and possibility.

> *"We missed it then, but it doesn't matter:*
>
> *tomorrow we will run faster,*
>
> *stretch out our arms farther ...*
>
> *and then one fine morning ...*
>
> *So we beat on,*
>
> *boats against the current,*
>
> *borne back ceaselessly into the past."*
>
> *[Francis Scott Fitzgerald, The Great Gatsby]*

When did we lose interest in the world?

When did we put on headphones and, lost in our notes, stopped listening to their sounds?

When did we allow our fingers to nurture bonds by stroking keys and no longer excited faces?

When did we stop listening to the voice of our ego, suffocating it with that of our thousand commitments?

I will not be happy if, at the end of the day, I have checked the list of my interminable duties but if even today, more than yesterday, I have taken a step to get a little closer to myself. Here, in the center of my breath. So good at feeling the weight of our duties.

Work, family, children, deadlines, home.

What kind of day is a day that hasn't seen even the shadow of a smile from you?

Taking the time to do what you like is at the end of your priority ladder. You almost can't tell without feeling guilty.

—I have no time—.

—Here, there is a lot to do. We can't stop—.

The day is over, and tomorrow we start again.

—The holidays, I'll wait for the holidays—.

To then start over. Again and again.

—There will be time, there will be a way—.

And in the meantime, the years fly by.

In the age of productivity and efficiency at any cost, your pleasure has become a luxury, a detail.

What value are you giving to your time?

Give yourself time, give yourself a moment. Get it, tear it, steal it from the trouble of your days.

May each dawn reveal a new desire,

may every night sleeps on your pillow

the echo of a smile

for that petal of beauty

that you stole

to the day now gone.

If Not Now, When?

How much part of you is still in the past, mulling over —what would have been if—, your choices, the missed possibilities, what you consider mistakes today?

All this represents an intense energy charge that you disperse into something that cannot change by now.

Does it make sense to judge our choices afterward? There was a time, that time when your choice was the one you took, with the elements you had then.

Or maybe you haven't even asked yourself, postponing thoughts and doubts to a—tomorrow—that sooner or later would come to ask for the bill. And today?

Over the years, you have felt your tomorrow fading, and that—yesterday—getting heavier every day.

But between yesterday and tomorrow, there is—today—.

This moment, too often crushed and mortified between two now inconsistent temporal spaces; yesterday is gone, and—tomorrow there is no certainty—.

In 10 years, you will also place this moment in the heavy burden of—what it would have been if—. And in the meantime, life goes on, and our days are certainly not infinite.

Stop. Take back your present, the only real space full of possibilities.

The abode of choice is today.

Not yesterday, not tomorrow.

So? If not now, when?

Closing Credits

Last chapter.

It always comes to an epilogue.

To a break.

To an end.

I tried to tell how to do it to a dear friend, to someone you want to take care of.

I tried to make sense of the thoughts dancing in my head. I hope I succeeded.

I hope I have come to touch some strings.

Some hidden point of your heart, of your soul.

Because basically, the strength of thought is precisely this, to reach beyond distances, wherever there is someone able to perceive it.

What if you knew that yours are the last steps?

That shortly the possibilities so long postponed will no longer be possible, that is no longer time to say,

—maybe tomorrow, another day—,

that the hourglass is now almost empty,

that the setting sun lowers the curtain of a night that will never end.

If you knew all of this, now, at this very moment,

are you really sure you are who, where, and whom you want?

The days are not infinite, and—tomorrow—can be the self-made trap of an endless alibi.

Waiting for a Godot who won't come if we don't get him.

A great mystic was dying. His disciples, pressed to his bedside, asked him, "Master, what is your last message?" The Master gathered his last strength, opened his eyes, and pointed to the roof of his hut with his index finger.

A squirrel was playing.

All the disciples looked upwards, and for an instant, there was absolute silence. The Master spoke in a faint voice.

He said, "This is the message of my whole life. Live in the moment. It's wonderful to hear the squirrel playing on the roof without worrying about anything else."

And he added, "Now, I can die."

And he died with a smile on his lips and a face full of bliss.

And then nothing. That's all.

Like everything that exists, this short journey of ours together ends here. Then each will continue his own.

Now breathe, move your body slowly, feel the energy that pleasantly animates your senses.

Then look up beyond these pages. And look

The road to happiness can be *your* road to happiness.

Here, now.